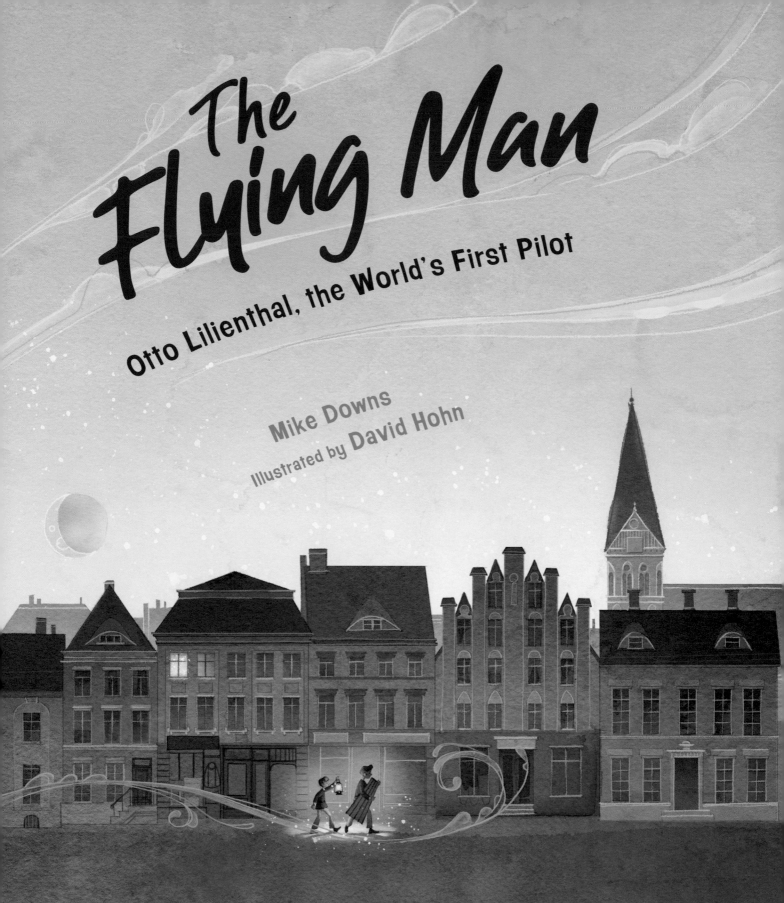

The Flying Man

Otto Lilienthal, the World's First Pilot

Mike Downs

Illustrated by David Hohn

ASTRA YOUNG READERS

AN IMPRINT OF ASTRA BOOKS FOR YOUNG READERS
New York

For Dad. Thank you for your constant love and support. And a special ALOHA for settling in Hawaii during my formative years!—*MD*

For Moon. Your constant support made this book happen.—*DH*

ACKNOWLEDGMENTS
A special thanks to: Sarah Venditti, who helped this project get started; to Johannes Fuchs, an amazing translator whose professionalism, insight, and boundless enthusiasm made this book possible; and Peter Busse and Bernd Lukasch, the current and former directors of the Otto Lilienthal Museum in Anklam, Germany, whose expertise and knowledge helped make this book as accurate as it could be.

PICTURE CREDITS
Back cover photo and images 1, 3, 4, and 5 in the Path to Flight spread are courtesy of the Archives of the Otto Lilienthal Museum. Image 2 in the spread is courtesy of the public domain.

For information about permission to reproduce selections from this book, please contact permissions@astrapublishinghouse.com.

Astra Young Readers
An imprint of Astra Books for Young Readers, a division of Astra Publishing House
astrapublishinghouse.com
Printed in China

ISBN: 978-1-63592-550-0 (hc)
ISBN: 978-1-63592-551-7 (eBook)
Library of Congress Control Number: 2021918485

First edition
10 9 8 7 6 5 4 3 2 1

Design by Barbara Grzeslo
The text is set in Futura Std Medium.
Illustrations are done in digital watercolor, colored pencils and gouache and rendered in Photoshop.

Otto's breath came in ragged gasps as he struggled up the slope. A pair of huge wings weighed heavily on his arms. Twice the fourteen-year-old had dashed downhill, leaping and flapping. Twice the force of gravity had held him earthbound, crushing his dream of soaring skyward.

Otto trudged up the last few feet as stars sparkled above his hometown of Anklam, Germany. He and his brother Gustav, who was almost a year and a half younger, practiced flying at night so nobody would laugh at them.

Otto stretched his weary arms. He must flap harder. Run faster. Jump higher. He wanted to fly like the storks that he and Gustav studied. If they could leap into the air with flapping wings, then so could he!

He took one—two—three quick steps and raced back down the slope.

Night after night, Otto and Gustav attempted to fly.

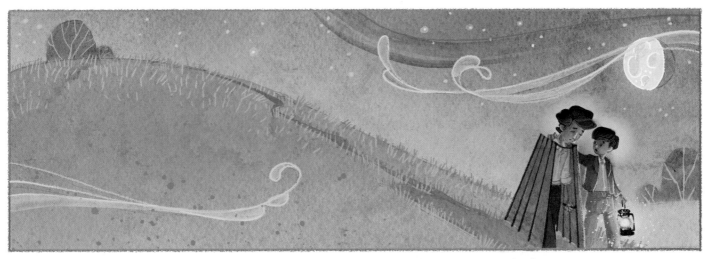

Night after night, exhausted and disappointed, they returned home.

In 1862, balloons were the only way people could reach the sky. Otto didn't want to float in balloons. He wanted to soar like a bird.

Scientists, teachers, and news reporters everywhere said flying was impossible. He desperately wanted to prove them wrong.

Even though his first attempts had failed, he wouldn't give up.

When it was clear that the wings weren't going to work, the brothers stored them away and came up with a new plan. They would build a huge man-size flapping machine. That would surely lift them into the sky!

School and work filled their days, so it took four long years before their finished flapping machine hung in their attic, ready for testing. It was a fantastic invention of straps and pulleys and feather-stitched wings. The pilot's arms and legs were connected by ropes to power the wings. When flapping up, the wings opened like shutters. When flapping down they snapped shut to push against the air.

Otto strapped himself in. *Today* he would fly!

Whoosh! Otto forcefully pushed his legs and arms outward. The wings beat down against the still air. The machine began to lift the tiniest bit! Was he about to fly?

No! When the wings beat down, the apparatus would rise a few inches, but when the wings moved up, the whole machine would drop, hanging at the end of a taut rope. *Oomph!*

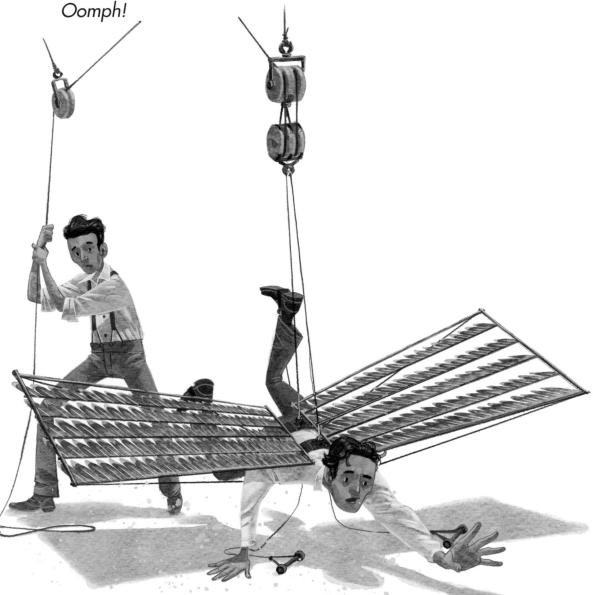

Gustav and Otto tried again and again. No matter how hard they struggled and strained, they couldn't make it fly.

Eventually, they gave up on their machine ever soaring into the air.

But they didn't give up on flying!

The brothers sketched and planned for another two years. They built a new machine—this time it had six wings. It was so large, they had to build it in their uncle's barn instead of inside their attic. When it was finally ready, they hung it outside for testing.

Their uncle thought they were wasting their time.

Friends thought they were crazy to believe anyone could *ever* fly.

The brothers ignored them all.

Otto strapped himself into the machine. He pumped
furiously with his legs on the stepping device that
powered the wings. This time, the extra wings pushed
harder against the air. Otto felt himself starting to rise.
But he couldn't flap the wings hard enough to lift the
machine by much, and it took so much effort that any
lift only lasted a few seconds. Gustav took turns with
Otto, but he couldn't make it fly, either.

Once again . . . the machine hung flightless at the end of the rope.

People wondered why the brothers kept trying. Making a flying machine was impossible!

Were they right? Was flying impossible?

No! Somehow, Otto would find a way to prove them wrong.

It would be months before he figured out how.

The answer came to him one day as he watched a stork soar gracefully overhead. That was it! He needed to *glide* first, not flap.

Otto and Gustav gave up on flapping machines. They decided to build something that would glide instead. Unfortunately, the brothers had to spend most of their time earning a living. Otto worked as an engineer. Gustav designed buildings. But on every vacation, they continued to test new ideas.

They tested small flying models and large kites.

They studied birds and experimented with different wing shapes.

They discovered that birds' wings had a special curved shape. Could *that* be the secret to flight?

It was twenty years before Otto and Gustav built another full-size flying machine. This time, they built a giant wing with space in the middle for a pilot's head and shoulders to fit through. Handles were attached underneath so the pilot could hold on to the wing.

Would the wing's special curved shape make the difference?

A fresh breeze shifted to and fro as the brothers carried their wing to a field. Otto held one side, keeping it steady. Gustav stood in the center of the wing, ready to fly.

Suddenly, a gust tore across the field blasting the wing with dust and rushing air.

Whoosh! Without any effort on Gustav's part, the wing lifted so powerfully that Otto couldn't hold on. It soared up into the sky, then slammed to the earth. Gustav flew from the machine, landing headfirst on the ground.

The brothers learned an important lesson that day— flying could be dangerous!

After that, Otto did most of the flying. But he practiced out of the wind.

He started by running and jumping off a board a few feet high. Doing that, he could fly about ten feet forward.

He practiced up to fifty times per day.

At first the wing didn't do what he wanted. It tilted and turned and twisted. But day by day, week by week, he learned to control it by shifting his weight back and forth.

Finally, he decided to test it back in the wind.

Otto carried his new wing to the top of a gentle slope. A breeze brushed against him as he peered down the hill. He took one—two—three quick steps. The weight of the glider disappeared as the wing lifted him skyward. He grinned. He shouted. He whooped with delight. This new joy of flying was something that no one else could claim.

But he wasn't completely in control yet. He soared through a swirl of air that sent him turning sideways. Otto fought to straighten the glider, but the wind was too strong. The wing fell dangerously low. It slammed into the grassy hill. Otto and his glider tumbled roughly to the ground.

Even with all his studying, he still had a lot to learn about flying.

As he practiced, he learned. . . .

If the wind pushed him from behind . . . *Crash!*

If he didn't move quickly enough to control the glider . . . *Crash!*

If a gust shoved him rapidly skyward, he had to let go before he got dangerously high. . . . *Crash!* . . . went Otto. *Crash!* . . . went the glider.

In time, Otto's flights got longer. His control got better. He crashed less and less as he learned the tricks and twists of the wind. He loved the breathtaking freedom! He loved the thrill of the earth dropping away.

Curious bystanders began to watch. Children sometimes raced alongside as he flew downhill. Most people thought he was crazy. But Otto was still happy to tell them about the thrill of flying.

Learning to fly took up every moment Otto could find. He repaired broken gliders. He built new, improved versions. He practiced for days, months, and years.

Eventually, crowds formed to watch him fly. Photographers arrived to take pictures. Flight pioneers from around the world traveled to meet him. By the time he was forty-eight years old, Otto could fly like a soaring bird while others could only dream of flying.

On August 2, 1896, Otto stood atop the Rhinow Hills, gripping his glider comfortably. It was a biplane—a beautiful craft of white cotton stretched over a bamboo frame. The summer breeze tugged impatiently at his wings, beckoning him. Below, a crowd of spectators stood mesmerized. They had come to witness the impossible.

Otto watched puffy white clouds dance across clear blue skies. He waited patiently as a pocket of gusty air swirled by.

Finally, the shifting breeze rushed toward him.

He took one—two—three quick steps. And the glider soared upward.

The hill disappeared beneath his feet.

A camera clicked, capturing the incredible sight. Screaming children chased headlong after him, tumbling down the hill. Most spectators stood speechless, mouths agape. Otto flew above them all with the rush of warm summer air singing through the glider's wings.

The newspapers described it best with the nickname
they gave him. No longer was he Otto Lilienthal,
engineer. After a lifetime of work and dreams, he was
now Otto Lilienthal . . .

. . . "The Flying Man."

Trial and Error
THE PATH TO FLIGHT

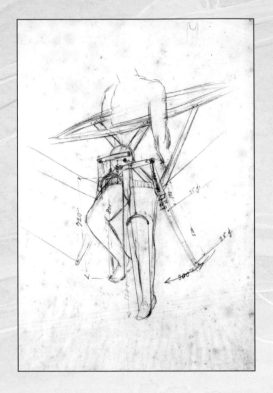

When Otto Lilienthal taught himself to fly, there were no books or instruction manuals on flight. He and Gustav had to figure everything out by themselves. They first tried to fly by making wings that flapped. They even devised a flapping machine that used their legs for added power.

It took years until they realized that flapping wouldn't work. Their arms and legs, even working together, couldn't produce enough power to lift them off the ground. Otto and Gustav finally decided they should try gliding instead of flapping. They spent the next many years studying the shapes of bird wings. These special shapes unlocked the secrets of flight.

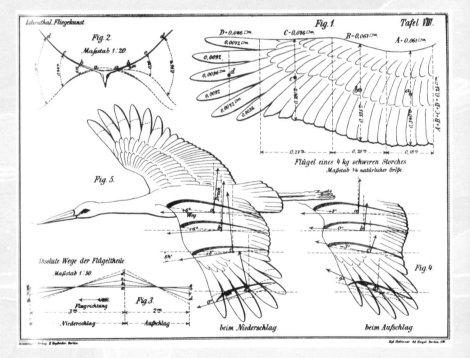

In the beginning, Otto attempted flights using only a wing. As he practiced and learned more about flying, he discovered that a wing alone was difficult to control. Soon, he began designing all his gliders with vertical and horizontal stabilizers (the tail parts).

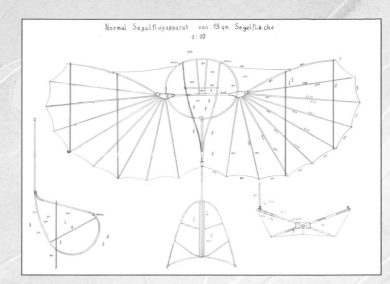

Otto practiced flying as much as he could. But he had a problem. Moving his glider to his favorite flying spots was difficult. He invented a solution by designing wings that folded. This allowed him to easily fit his glider on a train or cart for transportation.

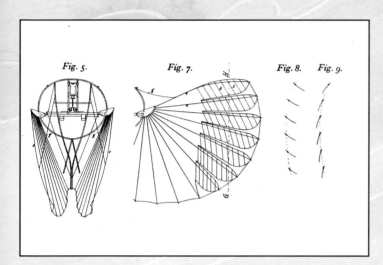

Otto always dreamed of staying aloft by using an engine. Airplanes today use propellers or jet engines to push them forward. But Otto still thought flapping was the answer. He designed gliders that had flappable wing "feathers" on the end of the glider wing. He also spent time designing an engine powerful and light enough to flap the feathers. Unfortunately, Otto never had the chance to test this idea.

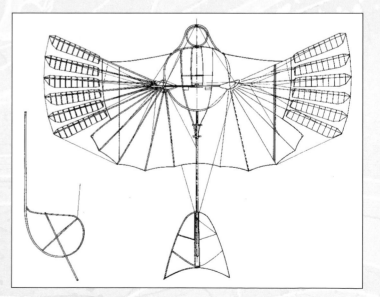

AFTERWORD

The Wright Brothers cited Otto Lilienthal as their greatest inspiration. If they had not read about his incredible achievements, it's likely they never would have invented the powered airplane. Orville and Wilbur Wright used Lilienthal's proven method of learning to fly. They tested wing shapes first, then used a step-by-step process as they learned to glide. They made over 1,000 glider flights before attempting to fly with an engine.

Gustav Lilienthal never attempted to fly after the crash he had when carrying the first wing. Otto Lilienthal never had the chance to fly with an engine, although that was his greatest goal. A week after the last flight described in this story, he flew into turbulent air and crashed to the ground. Sadly, he died of his injuries the next day.

More than seven years after Lilienthal's death, the Wright Brothers made their historic flights in the world's first powered airplane on December 17, 1903.

AUTHOR'S NOTE

My life has always been filled with flying—hang gliders, fighter jets, sailplanes, and airliners. But it wasn't until I began writing books that I made an interesting observation. I realized that whenever anyone talked about the beginnings of flight, they started with the Wright Brothers. But I began to wonder who came before them? Had anyone ever made repeated, controllable flights in a plane *without* an engine? Had anyone ever confidently flown time after time? Ultimately, I was asking: *who was the world's first pilot?*

This seemingly simple question guided me into a year of in-depth research and fascinating history. Since I have lived my life around aviation, I had a cursory knowledge of Otto Lilienthal. To begin my research, I went online and searched around the world for any books about Lilienthal, as well as books about early aviation. I found writings by Otto Lilienthal, his brother-in-law Gerhard Halle, the Wright Brothers, Octave Chanute, and several others. I quickly discovered why so few people in the United States know about him: most of the biographies, books, articles, and notes were written in German, the language of the country Otto lived in. Fortunately, I also found an incredible translator, Johannes Fuchs, who ended up becoming as passionate about this story as I was. Without him, I could never have accessed the material to write this book.

One way we're able to see Otto's achievements is through archival photos, especially those housed at the website of the Otto Lillienthal Museum in Anklam, Germany. I'm grateful Lilienthal was astute enough to encourage photographers to authenticate his achievements while he proved to the world that people could fly.